Save Our Planet: 52 Easy Things Kids Can Do Now

Save Our Planet:

52 Easy Things Kids Can Do Now

by Susan A. Levine
Illustrations by John Speirs

Parachute Press, Inc.
156 Fifth Avenue
New York, NY 10010

ISBN: 0-938753-35-5

First printing: October 1990
Printed in Canada

This book is printed on recycled paper.

Design by Gill Speirs

Contents

Air Actions

Animal Actions

Earth Actions

"For Kids Only" Actions

Introduction: Time for a Change

There's no place like Earth. It's the only planet in this solar system where we can breathe the air and walk around without a spacesuit! Our planet has been an orbiting life-support system for hundreds of millions of years.

People, on the other hand, have only been around for about 100,000 years. Yet today there are more of us than any other animal, fish, or bird. And a lot of our daily habits are adding up to big trouble for the planet:

♦ Our car habit is fouling Earth's air.

♦ Our throw-away habit is dirtying Earth's water.

♦ Our expensive habits (like wearing fur coats and ivory jewelry) are threatening Earth's other animals.

But there's something we can all do to save Earth—change our habits.

And changing our habits means taking action against pollution—action that starts small, like sorting garbage and riding bikes. With thousands of people doing it, we'll have a cleaner and healthier planet.

Saving the planet isn't an easy job—it won't happen overnight. It will take time for all of us to decide to change our habits and put a little Earth Action into our lives. But it's happening already, and it's happening all over the world.

What's Earth Action? It's when parents stop buying apples and apple juice sprayed with an unhealthy chemical called Alar. It's when people vote for politicians who put the planet's health before company or individual profits. And it's when kids start a save-the-planet club and convince their school to recycle paper.

More people than ever are working to make Earth a cleaner, safer place. You can join them. On nearly every page of this book, you'll find at least one way *you* can help save the planet. Choose a few to start with and put a little Earth Action in your life today!

Garbage Actions

Garbage Gridlock

Did you ever stop to think that *all* the garbage on Earth comes from people? No other earthlings throw things away. A quick look at the paper plates, plastic foam cups, plastic pudding containers, and juice boxes in any supermarket gives you an idea of a few of the things we use once and then throw away.

When it comes to garbage, the good old U.S.A. leads the way. Each American throws away about 3.5 pounds of garbage a day. That means nearly 1,277 pounds of garbage per person per year. A little more garbage math yields 320,000,000,000—that's 320 *billion*—pounds of U.S. garbage every year. You'd need over 7 million Statues of Liberty to equal what all that garbage weighs.

That's just the top of the global garbage iceberg. The rest of the world's population makes their share of garbage, too. And we're running out of places to put it—*no one* wants a garbage dump in his or her backyard! But we're still making a lot of garbage. In fact, one garbage dump in New York City is piled so high that by the year 2005 it will be taller than the Great Pyramid of Egypt!

The answer to Garbage Gridlock is change—change in our throw-away habits. That means remembering the three R's of garbage every day:

♦ Recycle glass, plastic, paper, aluminum, and tin.

♦ Re-use plastic bags as well as glass and plastic bottles and jars.

♦ Re-think what we mean when we say "garbage."

These changes start with one small act, and here it is:

Action #1. Take Your Daily Garbage Total

Tallying what you toss is the first thing to do in acting against Garbage Gridlock. When you see your Daily Garbage Total (DGT), you'll be able to cut down on the number of things you throw away every day.

Step 1. Take a sheet of paper and write Daily Garbage Total (DGT) across the top. Use the left side to list every hour of the day, starting with the hour you get up in the morning and ending with your bedtime. Use a ruler to divide the page so each hour has its own line. Write the days along the top and use a ruler to make columns.

Step 2. Pick a day to start watching your garbage. Use the DGT chart to keep an accurate record. If you toss a banana peel at breakfast, write it down in the right time slot. If you throw away a Styrofoam® tray or a plastic fork at lunch, write it down. By bedtime, you'll have an hour-by-hour breakdown of what you threw away when.

Step 3. Study your DGT. Count the number of apple cores, paper towels, empty juice boxes, cold french fries, broken pencils, old pizza, and other items you threw away. Then do a little garbage math. Multiply your DGT by 5—the number you get will be your average garbage total for any 5 days. You'll be amazed to see how much garbage you make! Keep reading for ways to cut down on all that garbage!

Recycling

Are any of these items on your Daily Garbage Total (DGT) chart:

- scrap pieces of computer paper?
- empty soda cans?
- old pet food cans?
- old comic books?

These things aren't garbage—they're all re-runs. They can be recycled and cut out of your DGT.

Recycling is a big word in the 90's. It means taking something man-made and making it into

something new that people can use again.

♦ Old Coke cans are recycled into Pepsi, A&W, 7-Up, or Slice cans.

♦ Yesterday's newspapers become tomorrow's report cards and notebooks.

♦ Empty plastic soda bottles are transformed into the filling for ski jackets or sleeping bags.

Your town or school is probably recycling already—and not a moment too soon! Recycling is the best way we know for taking old paper, cans, and plastic bottles out of the Garbage Gridlock and turning them into new and useful products.

Action #2. Return Re-Runs

♦ Look up the number of the Mayor's office in the phone book. Call to find out what you can recycle and when. Towns usually collect certain re-runs on certain days. Write the information down so your re-runs will be waiting on recycle days.

♦ Cash in your re-runs. Take all returnable bottles and cans back to the store. You'll make a nickel on each *and* help save the planet.

Garbage for Gardens

Check your DGT again. Look for:

♦ banana peels
♦ apple cores
♦ carrot ends
♦ orange peels
♦ cold pizza
♦ uneaten cheese sandwiches.

Any fruit peels, cores, or food that isn't meat can be taken out of the garbage bag and piled outside on dirt. In about a year, the pile will turn into the best fertilizer around.

Any food that comes directly from nature is organic. That means it will break down into a rich material called compost if it's left outside in the sun and air. You can see compost every time you walk in the woods. Pick any spot on the forest floor. Clear away the leaves on top, and your fingers will find moist, dark dirt. That's compost. It's what's left of fallen leaves, old acorns, dead branches, and anything organic that's dropped to the ground.

Making a compost heap is a fun way to recycle. Compost is a great natural fertilizer. It's filled with nitrogen and phosphorus—two of plants' favorite foods.

Action #3. Create a Compost Heap

It's easy to start a compost heap, no matter where you live.

City Compost

Step 1. Find a coffee can or flowerpot. Pour a little soil on the bottom. Place it on a fire escape or in a window box that gets sunlight.

Step 2. Add any non-meat leftovers such as fruit peels, old vegetables, eggshells, ashes, coffee grounds, and wilted flowers.

Step 3. Add a little more soil every now and then. Stir the contents with a stick every two weeks. In a few months, you'll have a container of compost. Use it to nourish houseplants and gardens, or give your can as a gift to a friend with a garden.

Country Compost

Step 1. Find a sunny spot in your yard and spread some dirt on the ground.

Step 2. Add your compostable garbage. That means all the stuff you'd put in a city compost plus hay, grass clippings, and animal bedding if you have cows or horses.

Step 3. Throw some dirt on your heap and turn it over with a pitchfork every two weeks. Your compost will be ready to use in about a year.

Mail-o-Matic

Most products come wrapped in packaging. Toys, cameras, CDs, and even magazines come wrapped in plastic or plastic foam. This kind of trash takes forever to go away. Plastic and plastic foam stay in garbage dumps for centuries, slowly releasing the sometimes harmful chemicals they're made of until they finally disappear.

Before plastics and plastic foams came along people managed to wrap fragile items with newspaper and attach tags to clothes with pins. Stores and companies can use other items to do that today. But they won't change the way they package until people prove they want it that way. The best way to let them know is to send the packaging back!

Action #4. Make a Special Delivery!

Step 1. The next time you unwrap a present like a new CD or a catcher's mitt and end up with more to throw away than to keep, get a box or large envelope. Put the packaging inside and get your pen and pencil ready.

Step 2. Write a letter to the president of the company that makes the product, stating your opinion of all that packaging. Put your letter in the box or envelope with the packaging and mail it. You can always find the name of the company on the package. Your letter can read like this:

> *(your address here)*
>
> Dear Sir/Madam,
>
> I like your *(product name here)*. But I had to throw a lot of packaging away. I wonder why you can't sell your *(product name here)* wrapped in something that makes less garbage or can be recycled. Please write back and tell me what you think.
>
> Yours truly,
>
> *(Your name—here)*

Step 3. Send your package Third Class. It won't cost as much as First Class mail but it will still arrive in a few days.

YELLOW BUTTER

Yellow butter purple jelly red jam black bread

Spread it thick
Say it quick

Yellow butter purple jelly red jam black bread

Spread it thicker
Say it quicker

Yellow butter purple jelly red jam black bread

Now repeat it
While you eat it

Yellow butter purple jelly red jam black bread

Don't talk
With your mouth full!

Mary Ann Hoberman

Mind Your Manners

Be kind to your planet. Litter hurts. It's ugly, *and* it can harm wild animals. They get caught in plastic trash, cut on broken glass, and tangled in old string and wire.

Action #5. Pick It Up—Take It Away

Be on litter alert all the time.

♦ When you see litter on the ground, pick it up and throw it in the nearest garbage can.

♦ If your friends litter, tell them they dropped something and explain why it's important to put litter in its proper place—a garbage can.

♦ Take litter like candy wrappers or cans and mail it back to the company that makes it. Send a letter that tells them their customers are littering. Ask them to do something about it. You can find the addresses you need on the can, label, or wrapper.

♦ Sometimes it's hard to be on litter alert. There aren't always enough places in parks and forests to put your garbage. When you go on a picnic or a camping trip, bring empty plastic grocery bags from home to carry your trash to a garbage can. That way, you can have a great time at the beach or in the woods, and you won't leave a mess that will make someone else's vacation less pleasant. When you clean up, you're keeping a little bit of the planet clean and safe for animals. And you can do some easy recycling at home by rinsing out the plastic garbage bag so it can be used over and over again.

Trash Mash

You can get people to think and talk about Garbage Gridlock by creating artwork out of garbage. Your garbage masterpiece will show people how we need to rethink our throw-away habit. When people see what a single day's worth of garbage adds up to, they'll realize that they throw away too many pieces of scrap paper, half-eaten chicken legs, plastic bags, dog food cans, old carrots, and other garbage everyday. Then, we can hope they'll try to change their wasteful habits.

Action #6. Box Your Garbage

Step 1. Save all the garbage in your house from one day. That means everything that doesn't go into the compost pile.

Step 2. Get a cardboard box.

Step 3. Glue all the garbage into the box. Glue it to the top, to the bottom, to the sides, and to the back. You can even glue some of it outside the box, too. Arrange it in a shape or color pattern that you like.

Step 4. When it's finished, take it to school. Tell your class that it's made out of one day's worth of your family's garbage. Ask them to think about how much garbage *they* throw away every day. Ask them what they can do to cut down on garbage, too.

Saying It with Garbage!

Here's another way to make art out of garbage. Think about all the soda cans people don't recycle. They end up as litter, and that's a big part of the garbage problem. Here's a way you can turn these cans into jewelry.

Action #7. Wear a Can

Step 1. Find a can that someone threw on the ground. Take it home and wash it out with soap and hot water.

Step 2. Take a hammer, a brick, or a log, and smash the can until it's flat.

Step 3. Feel the crushed can carefully for sharp edges. Pound those down until they're safe.

Step 4. Glue a safety pin on the can, and start wearing it! When someone asks why you're wearing a can for a pin, tell them you want to show people that there are more creative things to do with cans than just tossing them in the trash.

Or you can buy a crushed can pin that's already made with no sharp edges. Send a check for $4.50 to CanWear, P.O. Box 22, Montgomery, VT 05470. List your first and second choices as to the kind of can you want, and the people at CanWear will fill your order.

Toxic Search

The word "toxic" is bad news. It means poison. Many everyday household products have ingredients that become toxic when they end up in garbage dumps. It's a good bet that you have some toxic products in your basement, kitchen, or garage.

You can find them by reading labels. Products like drain un-cloggers, rust removers, batteries, furniture polish, motor oil, and paint may have these words on their labels: Warning, Caution, Danger, or Poison. If you find these words, you have a product that can become toxic waste when it's poured down the drain, into the ground, or dumped into the garage.

Action #8. Make a Clean Sweep

Grab a grown-up and get going!

Step 1. Look in the garage, basement, kitchen, and bathroom for any product you're not using that has a toxic word on its label. Put these products in a box.

Step 2. Some towns have collection days for toxic items. Call the sanitation department in your town to find out how they suggest getting rid of the toxic box. A grown-up will know where to look in the phone book.

Step 3. If you can't find a way to safely dispose of some products, seal them carefully and send them back to the company that made them.

You'll find the address on the label.

A Cleaner Kind of Clean

There are plenty of cleansers and polishes that you can make at home that won't end up as toxic waste. The ingredients are probably in your kitchen right now. If you have a bottle of vinegar, you've got the best glass cleaner there is. And lemon juice is great for scouring a dirty counter. So is baking soda. With a little mixing, you can come up with homemade products that are as good as the ones you can buy in the store—and a lot safer!

Action #9. Write Away Right Away!

♦ Use these addresses to get more information on what you can use instead of toxic cleaning products:

Send $2.00 for a chart showing cleaning products you can buy or make that aren't toxic to: Clean Water Fund, New Jersey Environmental Federation, 808 Belmar Plaza, Dept. GM, Belmar, NJ 07719.

Send $2.75 for a wheel that shows hazardous wastes, how to get rid of them, and what to use around the house instead to: Environmental Hazards Management Institute, 10 Newmarket Road, P.O. 932, Durham, NH 03824.

♦ Send for a Seventh Generation Catalog. This shop-by-mail catalog has plenty of cleansers, detergents, and soaps that are safe for you and safe for the planet. Call 1-800-456-1177 to have the catalog sent to you.

All in the Family

Everyone in your family can help break Garbage Gridlock at home. It just takes someone to help them get started. That someone can be you.

Action #10. Start a Home Team

There's no team like the home team! Your whole family can get involved with recycling, reducing, and re-using in order to cut down on household garbage. Together you can find places to store re-runs until pick-up time. Together you can send packaging back to the people who make it. Together you can make your home, street, and neighborhood a cleaner place for everyone.

So don't leave your family in the dugout when you've gone to bat for Earth. Get everyone involved. Saving the planet is a team effort!

♦ Ask your family to keep track of their Daily Garbage Total. Then have a family meeting to decide how you can all cut down on waste.

♦ Invite your family to add to the compost pile. The more organic garbage you pile up, the more super soil you'll get.

♦ Assign points to different types of garbage. A banana peel could be worth 10 points because it's organic. A microwave meal could be worth 1 point because most of them come wrapped in so much packaging. Cottage cheese in a recyclable container might be worth 5 points.

♦ Offer a prize to the home team member who scores the most points for Earth!

Garbage Gold

A lot of what you throw away can be used by other people. Comic books that you're ready to toss out may complete another kid's collection. Toys you don't play with anymore could be fun for kids who don't have any toys at all. Clothes that don't fit you could keep a homeless kid warm in winter. Giving away goods like these is another way of recycling—when you stop using them, someone else starts.

Action #11. Don't Throw Away—Give Away

Step 1. Make a list of all the stuff in your closet and drawers that you don't want anymore. This could include clothes, shoes, books, magazines, comics, toys, games, and even old bicycles. Show the list to your parents and ask them if you can give those things away.

Step 2. Think about who could use the items on your list. Then use the phone book to call the library, hospital, and groups that help the homeless to find out if they'll take what you've got to give.

Step 3. Round up all your giveaways and put them in boxes. Write the name or place each box is going to right on the box.

Step 4. Choose a day when one of your parents can help you by dropping off your giveaways.

Dangerous Fun

Balloons and kites are pretty and fun to play with. But when *your* fun is done, trouble begins. Balloons and kite string can harm wild animals. Birds get tangled in string and aren't able to fly. Some animals like sea turtles eat deflated balloons—the balloons get stuck in the animal's stomach and cause it to starve. That's a terrible thing to have happen. Fortunately, it's easy to prevent.

Action #12. Don't Let Go!

♦ After a party, pop all the balloons and wind up the string. Make sure you throw the balloons away in a sealed bag so they won't fall out. Save the string from the balloons. You can recycle it by using it again.

♦ If you use helium-filled balloons, don't let them go. Hold on to them for a few days. The gas inside will slowly escape. When the balloon is flat, throw it away in a sealed bag and save the string.

♦ Fly kites carefully. Don't take chances by flying them near trees or tall buildings where they can get tangled up. Make sure you're in an open area so they won't get caught on anything you can't reach.

♦ Kite string can be used over and over again. Even tangled string is still good. Just work on untying the knots. If you can't, cut the knots out and throw them away in a sealed bag. Then tie what's left from one kite onto the ball of string of another one. The longer your kite string, the higher your kite can fly!

Plastic Patrol

It's waterproof, strong, long-lasting, and comes in all shapes and sizes. It's plastic and it's in everything from sandwich bags to hardhats. By the year 2000, all plastic could be recyclable. But until then, a lot of plastic is ending up as garbage. And tons of it are floating around in the oceans.

Plastic fishing nets, six-pack rings, and bags are causing trouble in our planet's seas. Seals, whales, fish, seabirds, and sea turtles get caught in them or try to eat them. Thousands of ocean birds, animals, and fish die every year from plastic pollution.

Action #13. Join the Big Clean

♦ Whenever you find six-pack rings littered around, take them home and snip all the rings. Then put the plastic scraps into a garbage bag that can be tied shut. This way, no animals can get messed up in your garbage.

♦ When you go to the beach, remember to pack up all your leftovers and take away with you whatever garbage you make during the day.

♦ Sign up to help clean a beach near you. You can find out how by writing to: Center for Marine Conservation, 1725 DeSales Street NW, Suite 500, Washington, D.C. 20036.

Paper Prowl, Part I

Paper towels are made from trees. People carelessly tear off handfuls of paper towels to wipe up a juice spill or clean the car windows. Then they toss them in the trash and often take some more to finish the job. What a waste!

If you have paper towels in your house, try

not to use them. Set an example that the rest of the family can follow. You can show them that paper towels aren't necessary. They're just a habit that's easy to break.

Action #14. Wipe Out Paper Towels

Step 1. Save old T-shirts, blue jeans, and towels.

Step 2. Wash them and dry them—on a line if you can. Dryers use electricity, and that makes pollution!

Step 3. Tear them into small, medium, and large pieces. Then store them in an old pillowcase or paper bag.

Step 4. Keep some rags in the garage, some in the kitchen, some more in the basement, and some in the bathroom. And put them anywhere else people might need to wipe something up.

Step 5. Start using the cloths instead of paper towels. When they get dirty, wash them out and use them again and again and again!

Paper Prowl, Part II

Many people use just one side of a piece of paper. Then they throw it away. Try this Earth Action Challenge: Get through a whole day without using one new blank piece of paper. By using your mind, you'll find plenty of other paper to write on!

Action #15. Get Pad Mad

♦ Cut up some brown paper bags. This heavy paper can be used to make posters or other projects in art class. Make a pad!

♦ Make a pad out of envelopes that come in the mail—they're almost always clean on the back. Just staple the pieces together so the blank sides face up.

Paper Prowl, Part III

Here's a song you and your friends can rap to show other kids how you feel about wrapping paper. If you don't like this one, write your own "wrap" rap and perform it with your friends.

Action #16. Do the Wrap Rap

We make too much garbage every day!
There's got to be a better way!

We have to think, got to use our minds
To come up with answers of all kinds!

Here's one way to say no to trash
Without spending any extra cash!

Forget wrapping paper! Don't spend
your money!
It's bad for Earth and it isn't funny!

Wrap gifts in Archie, if you can.
If you don't like that, use Superman
or the Wednesday paper or Seventeen—
Whenever you make the birthday scene.

It's not too hard, it's plenty of fun!
It's a way to get Earth Action done!

Wrapping paper doesn't have to be bad
And saving the planet is really rad!

Water Actions

Water Watch

Take a look at a globe and you'll see that there's much more water on our planet than there is land. Our vast seas and clouds are what makes Earth look like a big blue-and-white marble in photos taken from outer space.

Every pond, lake, river, and stream helps the planet's animals and plants stay alive. All life on Earth needs water to survive, yet most people take water for granted. We just turn on a faucet and there it is—plenty of clean, fresh water.

Water is a great place to play, too. If you've ever been lifted by a big wave at the beach or ridden in an inner tube down some gentle rapids, you know how much fun water can be. But Earth's water is in trouble. It's getting dirty fast from pollution and trash dumping.

Anything that affects the water affects life on Earth. So anyone who wants to help save the planet has to become a Water Watcher also.

Water that moves underground through dirt and around rocks is called groundwater. It rushes down hills after winter snows melt and after summer thunderstorms. Groundwater feeds Earth's springs, ponds, and rivers—and it's a big part of the water we drink.

Today's groundwater is moving through troubled turf. Too many industries and homes are dumping too much dangerous waste into our water.

Action #17. Become a Groundwater Guard

Even though you can't see it, you can protect groundwater from pollution.

♦ Everything dumped down the drain ends up in water somewhere. Lots of household cleaning products we pour down the drain can harm the groundwater. See Action #8 for more about these toxic products and how to get them out of your house.

♦ Dumping motor oil on the ground is bad for groundwater. Don't let your parents do it!

♦ Some fertilizers and bug sprays are also bad for groundwater, too. See Action #44 for three natural ways to beat bugs in the garden.

Runaway Water

Most families waste more water than they use. It's easy to see why. Just watch your family's water habits for one day. Does anyone leave the water running while they brush their teeth, wash the dishes, or wait for the water to get really cold? Do people take long showers? If the answer is yes, hundreds of gallons of water are going down your drain everyday.

Action #18. Master the Tap

♦ Make a list of all the ways you use water. Your list will show you how often you turn on the tap without thinking of how much water is being wasted.

♦ Turn off the faucet while you're brushing your teeth. That saves about a gallon a day.

♦ Soap up dirty dishes with the water off. Just use a hot, soapy sponge instead of running water over every dish. Then turn on the tap to rinse everything clean. That could save about 20 gallons a day.

♦ Running water to get an icy cold drink wastes about 3 gallons. Wash out an empty jar—a big peanut butter jar is the perfect size. Fill it with water and keep it in the refrigerator. The next time you need an icy cold, thirst-quenching drink, it'll be waiting for you.

♦ Wear a waterproof watch. Time how long it takes you to shower. Then start cutting down on shower time day by day. You might want to time the showers of the rest of your family, too. See who can set the house record for cleanest bod/shortest showers.

Wise Water Ways

With a little creativity, you can help save water every day. There are plenty of ways for cutting down on the water that comes into and goes out of your home.

Action #19. Be a Drip Detective

♦ Leaks can drip, drip, drip away hundreds of gallons of water a day. Check all faucets and hoses in your house or apartment. If you find any leaks, tell a grown-up. It might mean tightening a bolt, buying a new hose, or even calling a plumber. But any money that's spent will come back as savings on the water bill.

♦ The average family of four sends 100 gallons of mostly clean water a day down the toilet. You can be flushbuster and cut that number down easily. Get a grown-up to help you lift the cover off the back of the toilet. Carefully put a brick or a plastic bottle filled with rocks on the bottom of the tank. The brick or bottle takes up room and cuts down on the amount of water it takes to fill the tank.

♦ Make an Insta-Wet Plant Watering *System*.

Step 1. First fill an empty plastic bottle with water.

Step 2. Turn the bottle over and push it into a potted plant or window box. Don't panic! A lot of water will rush out at first.

Step 3. When the dirt is wet, the water that's left in the bottle will trickle out very slowly, day by day, to quench the plants' thirst. This saves energy *and* water, and it's a creative way to recycle a plastic bottle!

Back to the Future

Years ago, before pipes and pumps brought running water everywhere, people drank rainwater. They also used rainwater to water their gardens. You can use rainwater today while conducting a scientific experiment at the same time.

Action #20. Make a Rainwater Reserve

Step 1. Save a large plastic container like an empty milk jug or gallon soda bottle. Get a grown-up to help you cut off the narrow top so you have a wide, open mouth on the container.

Step 2. Get a ruler and a magic marker or grease pencil to mark off every quarter inch up to 10 inches.

Step 3. Place the container on a window box or a level part of your yard. The next time it pours, you can measure how much rain falls. You can even keep a rain log and write the amount

on the calendar. Check the accuracy of your rain gauge by listening to the local weather report to see much rain they say fell.

Step 4. When your container reaches the top, use the water to give a thirsty plant a cool drink. This water is for plants only—not for you!

Stream Support

Is there running water in your neighborhood? Not the kind in pipes, but the natural kind—in brooks, streams, or swamps. If you answer "yes" to this question, you have a chance to take care of a small but important part of the planet.

Action #21. Start a Clean Stream Team

Get your friends and neighbors together and adopt a stream, pond, or riverbank. That means taking the time to walk by every few days to watch out for its well-being. Don't taste the water. Use your other senses to make sure the water is A-okay.

♦ What color is the water? Does it smell clean or dirty? Can you see fish and plants in it? Healthy streams of clear, moving water are usually filled with fish and insects. Unhealthy water smells like rotten eggs, has suds or oil on it, and can have an odd orange, red, or bright green color.

♦ If the stream is clean, keep it that way. Pick up any litter you see on the ground. Write City Hall to get a trash can placed nearby. Make your own signs that tell people to keep the area clean. If the stream is dirty and smells funny, act fast. Report your findings to your teacher and your class. Get their help in writing to politicians, calling reporters, and digging around to find out who is making the water dirty.

♦ For more help in adopting a stream, write to: The Izaak Walton League, 1401 Wilson Boulevard, Level B, Arlington, VA 22209. Ask for their free Save Our Streams booklet.

Air Actions

Breathe Deep

Earth's got great air. Our oxygen–carbon dioxide–nitrogen mix is a perfect blend to support life as we know it. If you were to take a deep breath on Venus, you'd inhale toxic gases like sulfuric acid. Over on Jupiter, the atmosphere has methane and ammonia in it. Here on Earth, methane heats homes and ammonia is a health hazard!

The air is one of Earth's gifts. For hundreds of thousands of years, Earth's atmosphere has been clean and healthy. But since people started burning coal, oil, and gas, Earth's air has become polluted.

We've been burning these fuels for about 150 years. They power our cars, factories, homes, and schools. Our fuel habits have to change in order to save the planet's air supply.

The number-one cause of air pollution is making electricity. So any way you can change your electricity habit means less air pollution, too!

Action #22. Turn "On" Off!

♦ Every time you turn off a light, you're cutting down on air pollution. Turn "on" off at home when you leave a room, and do it at school, too. Just ask your teacher first!

♦ If your classroom gets a lot of sunlight, ask the teacher to turn some lights off and use sunpower instead of fuel power.

♦ All lightbulbs are not created equal. Some use less energy and burn longer than others. You can find these lightbulbs in the Seventh Generation Catalog. To order a copy, call 1-800-456-1177.

♦ Let your hair dry naturally instead of using a blow-dryer. In the summer, use solar power to dry your hair. In other words, stand out in the sun until your hair dries!

♦ The sun can do a lot more than dry hair. People have begun using batteries that turn sunlight into power. These solar batteries can run cars and heat homes. Some people think that solar power is the power of the future. For information about solar power, write to: Solar Energies Industries Association, Suite 610, 1730 North Lynn Street, Arlington, VA 22209-2209.

Inventor's Corner

Why wait for the future? Put on your thinking cap today and invent something solar for tomorrow. Be creative and have fun! Can you think of an awesome design for a solar-powered turbo sports car? How about a solar powered computer or a toy that never needs batteries because it runs on sunpower? Turn your mind to the sun and see what you can invent!

Action #23. Go Solar!

Step 1. Get ready to invent. All you need is a pad, some crayons, and your own brain.

Step 2. Think of an item you use everyday or make up something new you'd like to be able to own.

Step 3. Draw it, name it, and show in your artwork how it gets its power from the sun.

Step 4. When you're finished, share your drawing and your idea with your friends or your classmates. That's a good way to get them thinking about solar power, too!

Step 5. Send your idea to a company you think might make what you've invented some time in the future. If you've drawn a solar car, send your drawing to: Office of the President, General Motors Corporation, Detroit, MI 48202. If you have a colored toy on the drawing board, send it to: Office of the President, Mattel, Inc., 5150 West Rosecrans Avenue, Hawthorne, CA 90250. Solar computer inventors can mail their ideas to: Office of the President, IBM, Old Orchard Road, Armonk, NY 10504.

Traffic Jam

Cars run on oil and gas and they are the number-two producer of air pollution. No matter how "clean" the gasoline, the 400 million cars people drive around the world still spew harmful chemicals into the air. No country has more cars than the United States. Today, there are enough trucks and cars on the road in the U.S.A. to drive a total of two trillion miles in one year. That's enough mileage to drive to Pluto and back 364 times!

By the year 2035, Earth's oil reserves will probably be gone. By then, there will be new ways to power cars. But an old way of getting around is looking better and better—the future just may be filled with bicycles!

Action #24. Use Pedal Power

Riding bikes is a great way to save the planet. Bicycles don't pollute, and the person providing the power will get in great shape!

♦ Start slowly. Buy a bike helmet and use your bike for small trips like going to a nearby store or a friend's house. As you get into better shape, go for longer rides. Contact your local police for information on bike safety.

♦ Start a bike club on your block. Get other kids to kick the car habit and start riding together. Why not ride to a park for a picnic? Just don't leave your garbage behind!

♦ For more information on cars and clean air, write to: National Clean Air Coalition, 1400 16th Street NW, Washington, DC 20036.

The People-Tree Connection

Planting trees can help save the planet. Trees are home for birds and small animals. Fruit and nut trees provide sweets and treats. And trees are the *only* places in the world to build tree houses.

Trees also help cut down on air pollution. They do this by taking the number-one cause of air pollution, carbon dioxide, out of the air. Trees absorb carbon dioxide through their leaves and use it, along with sunlight and water, to grow. To top that off, trees put oxygen back in the air. Since people need oxygen to breathe, we need trees to get along!

Action #25. Plant a Tree

♦ Make tree planting part of any celebration from birthdays to graduations to the 4th of July!

♦ Do some research. There are hundreds of trees to choose from. Borrow a book about trees from the library and find out which ones grow in your part of the country. Or talk to neighbors who have lots of trees on their land. Ask them which ones grow best.

♦ Join the National Arbor Day Foundation. It only costs $1.00 and you get a free tree. Once you're a member, you can buy all kinds of trees for under $5.00 each. To join, send your dollar to: National Arbor Day foundation, 100 Arbor Avenue, Nebraska City, NE 68410.

♦ The American Forestry Association wants

to plant 100 million trees around the United States by 1992. To see how you can help them reach that goal, send for a Citizen's Action Guide. Write to: Global ReLeaf, P.O. Box 2000, Washington, D.C. 20013 (1-202-667-3300).

♦ If you live in a city, adopt a tree. Call your Department of Parks and Recreation and find out how. Their number is in the phone book. Ask a grown-up to help you find it.

Tree Planting: A Step-by-Step Guide

When you finally have your tree, here's how to plant it:

Step 1. Choose a sunny spot where water doesn't puddle up after a storm. Too much water can cause the young tree's roots to rot.

Step 2. Dig a hole deeper than the roots and wider than the tree. Break up the soil around the hole so the tree's roots can push out and down as it grows.

Step 3. Place the tree inside the hole so the part just above the roots will be above the dirt.

Step 4. Spread the roots around and start filling the hole with the soil you dug up. It's a good idea to mix the fill with some compost (see Action #3).

Step 5. Press the dirt firmly around the roots so there are no air pockets. When the hole is almost filled, add water until it reaches the top. Then fill the hole with dirt and compost the rest of the way.

Step 6. Add more water and cover the filled hole with shredded bark. That helps keep moisture in. Now watch your tree grow from year to year!

Tree Years Old

Here's another idea. Plant your tree on your birthday or your sister's birthday or your grandmother's birthday. Every time one of you becomes a year older, so will your tree!

A Living Christmas

Every year, millions of trees are cut down so people can have Christmas trees. Most of those trees end up in garbage dumps. This year, try something different and keep your holiday tree growing all year long!

Action #26. Buy a Live Tree

Step 1. Look for a Christmas tree growing in a pot or one that has all its roots wrapped in a sack.

Step 2. Keep the tree outside until Christmas. Decorate it and celebrate the holiday around the tree as usual.

Step 3. When Christmas is over, water the tree and give it plant food once every two weeks.

Step 4. In the spring, plant your ex–Christmas tree in your yard (see Action #25). Next Christmas, decorate your tree outside!

Rainforests for Life

Tropical rainforests are warm, moist jungles with more plants, flowering vines, trees, and animals than any other place on Earth. They're filled with parrots, frogs, butterflies, monkeys, and leopards.

Earth's tropical rainforests are found in some of the warmest places including Central and South America, Africa, and Indonesia. The only tropical rainforests in the U.S.A. are in Hawaii—

and they're in trouble. The size of Earth's rainforests is getting smaller every year. That's because people are destroying them. They're burning huge areas of the rainforests to the ground in order to make room for cattle ranches. They're cutting down giant trees daily and turning the wood into lumber, furniture, and paper. Every hour about 3,000 acres of rainforest are destroyed. At that pace, all the tropical rainforests will be gone in 100 years.

What makes this bad news worse is that we can't replant a rainforest. Once it's cut down or burned, a rainforest is gone forever. That means fewer trees to take carbon dioxide out of the air and no homes for hundreds of rare birds and animals. People all over the world are working to save the rainforests. You can, too.

Action #27. Save the Rainforests

♦ For more information on the rainforests, write to: Rainforest Action Network, 301 Broadway, Suite A, San Francisco, CA 94133 (1-415-398-4404).

♦ Use recycled paper. That saves trees in the rainforest and around the world. Earth Care Paper Company has a catalog filled with recycled paper goods. To order a catalog, write to: Earth Care Paper Company, P.O. Box 3335, Madison, WI 53704.

♦ Adopt an acre of tropical rainforest. Your

class can get in on this idea and raise the money to help save an acre in Brazil. For information, write to: World Wildlife Fund/Canada, 60 St. Clair Avenue East, Suite 201, Toronto, Ontario M4T 1N5. You'll need a 45-cent stamp to mail a letter to Canada.

The No Zone

A part of Earth's atmosphere is in big trouble. It's the ozone layer. Ozone is a form of oxygen that's found about 30 miles above the planet's surface. Ozone acts like a giant umbrella—it keeps most of the sun's strongest rays off Earth. That's good for the planet. Without ozone, people could get badly sunburned and some plants and crops would be destroyed.

The ozone is in trouble because of chemicals called Chlorofluorocarbons, or CFCs. CFCs are used to help keep refrigerators cool. They also make spray cans spray and are used to make plastic foams such as Styrofoam.® When CFCs reach the air, they drift up through the atmosphere to the ozone layer. When the CFCs get there, they destroy the ozone.

Action #28. Say No to CFCs

♦ Don't use plastic foam. It's made with CFCs, and it's in a lot of everyday throw-away items. Watch out for plastic foam fast-food containers, soda cups, and egg cartons. Buy food and drinks that come in cardboard instead. Cardboard doesn't have any CFCs in it, and you can recycle it instead of throwing it away.

♦ Don't use spray cans. Spray cans use plenty of CFCs to send out spray. Buy pump-action spray bottles or try to find what you need in a jar.

♦ Air conditioners use CFCs to cool a room. Turning the family air conditioner on and off may not be up to you. But you can suggest that your family use the air conditioner only when it's really too hot inside. Ask everyone in the family to set the air conditioner on "low" and run it only long enough to cool the house down. And if you have a backyard with some shade, set up some chairs in a cool spot and ask everyone to cool off naturally.

Animal Actions

Home Sweet Home

There are thousands of animals on Earth. How many of them can you name? Get a piece of scrap paper and a watch. Give yourself 60 seconds to write down every animal you can think of. Chances are each of these animals needs your help in one way or another. That's because there are so many of us humans that our daily habits are harming the animals on our planet.

Our oil spills destroy birds' breeding grounds and ocean creatures' feeding grounds. Our factory smoke causes all kinds of pollution that harm animals' health—including our own! (Don't forget—we're animals, too.) Our throwaway habits create garbage dumps that pollute the water. The very clothes and jewelry some people wear mean death to other animals.

The good news is that there's a lot of save-the-animals action around the world. And you can start by helping to save the African elephants!

African elephants have been in the news a lot recently. It's a good thing, too. It made people see that elephants were being hunted to death for their tusks.

Tusks are made of ivory, and people around the world want ivory jewelry, chopsticks, boxes, statues, and piano keys.

Even elephants that lived in special parks weren't safe. Hunters called poachers broke the law and tracked them down. So many elephants were being killed for their tusks that it looked like they might be gone by the year 2000.

That's when the worldwide elephant action started. A meeting was called to try and save the elephant. People from the United States, France, Germany, and Switzerland were there. All the countries represented agreed not to let any ivory into their countries for two years.

So far, the ivory ban is having a good effect. The price of ivory has dropped way down. That means it's harder for poachers to make money killing elephants. The countries where elephants live are using soldiers in Jeeps and helicopters to protect the animals, and that makes it dangerous for poachers, too.

This has been a good start, but unless ivory is banned forever, the killing could start again. That's why now is a good time to get in on the elephant-saving action by connecting with people who are already making a difference.

Action #29. Join the Pachyderm Patrol

An elephant is also called a pachyderm. But no matter what you call it, keep on reading to find out how to help.

♦ The ivory ban in the United States ends in 1992. President George Bush is the man who can make it continue. Write to him, and tell him what you think of the ivory ban. His address is: The White House, 1600 Pennsylvania Avenue, Washington, D.C. 20501.

♦ Tell your teacher the World Wildlife Fund has classroom information about elephants. To find out about it, write to: World Wildlife Fund, 1250 24th Street NW, Washington, D.C., 20037.

♦ Be on the lookout for ivory. When you see people wearing ivory jewelry, ask them if they know where it comes from. Tell them that when it comes to ivory, you're on the elephant's side!

Manatees Need You!

Manatees are just like underwater cows—in fact, some people call them sea cows. They slowly swim along the bottom of warm, shallow beaches and graze for food. Instead of grass, manatees eat all kinds of seaweed and saltwater plants.

They can stay underwater for about fifteen minutes. Then, like whales, they come to the surface to breathe air. And like whales, manatee mothers nurse their babies and stay with them for a year. Manatees are large, gentle, and in trouble.

One of the feeding grounds of the Atlantic manatee is in waters just off the coast of Florida. These waters are crowded with people having a good time in their motorboats. The manatees get hurt by the boats and killed by their propellers.

They get caught in fishing lines and nets people let drift away. The water they swim in is being polluted.

People in Florida and around the U.S.A. want to save the manatee. You can help them.

Action #30. Be My Manatee

♦ Adopt a manatee. For $15.00 a year, your class or family can help Florida look after the manatees in trouble. You'll learn your manatee's name and receive news about its health and safety. For more information, call the Save the Manatee Club at the Florida Audubon Society at this number: 1-800-432-5646. They'll send you a newsletter. Read it and you'll find out who's helping the manatee in Washington, D.C., and in the state of Florida. You'll also learn who to write to in order to support laws that will protect manatees from motorboats.

Backyard Benefit

A backyard fair or garage sale can raise money to help your favorite animal. Here's how to set one up.

Action #31. Shop and Save

Step 1. Decide what animal you'd like to help. Then ask your family and friends to join you in an Animal Aid Sale to help that animal.

Step 2. Make posters about your Animal Aid Sale. Include facts about its habits and the trouble it's in. Don't forget to mention the day, time, and place.

Step 3. Set up everything you have for sale with price tags in the backyard or on the sidewalk. But first take a walk through a store to see what the items you're selling cost when they're brand new. Then cut that price in half when making your own tags.

Step 4. See Action #11 for more ideas about what you can sell.

Step 5. Make cookies and lemonade to sell to people who stop and shop.

Step 6. Tell everyone that the money you raise will go to helping that animal.

Step 7. For extra fun, you and your friends can even dress up as the animal and talk to people about your animal's problems.

Pet Pals

Is owning a pet acting to save the planet? The answer is yes if you take in a stray or an animal from a shelter.

Too many people fall in love with a cute kitten or puppy and bring it home only to ignore it a few weeks later. They don't feed it the right food. They don't care if it gets pregnant. And when they get angry, they take it out on their pet. That's why animal shelters are crowded with scared and lonely dogs and cats that need the right kind of person to take them home. Maybe you're the right kind of person.

Pets give people a chance to take care of one of Earth's animals for years and years. In exchange for food and shelter, pets offer us a lifetime of love and friendship.

Action #32. Plan an Adopt-a-Pet Day

Step 1. Find out the name and phone number of the nearest animal shelter.

Step 2. Call them up and ask how many cats and dogs, kittens and puppies they have. Explain that you would like to arrange an Adopt-a-Pet Day for your neighbors to meet at the animal shelter and look at the animals. Assure them that you and your friends will get everyone together and that all they have to do is prepare to have lots of people at the shelter at one time. Say that there's a good chance that many of them will want to adopt!

Step 3. Once you set aside the day, tell your neighborhood friends about the animals that need homes. Work together to make signs that tell people about Adopt-a-Pet Day: what it is and when and where it will take place. You can also send out or pass out flyers with the time, date, and place, as well.

Step 4. On Adopt-a-Pet Day, go to the animal shelter and help people decide whether or not to bring home a pet. Let them know how important it is that the animal gets lots of fresh air, healthy food, and love. If you'd like, talk to your own

family and decide if you want to have a pet. If you do, adopt one, too!

Fur Is for Animals

Fur coats are a symbol of money in today's world. They cost hundreds and even thousands of dollars. Men and women who wear fox or raccoon or mink or coyote coats say they want to spoil themselves. They say they love how soft and warm their coats are. They don't care that their furs were once a natural part of animals that were killed to make their coats—in fact, they're a lot like the people who buy ivory.

There was a time when people needed fur coats. Thousands of years ago, during the Ice Age, it was very, very cold. People had to hunt to survive. They filled their stomachs with meat and used almost every other part of the animals they killed. Skin and fur became shoes, coats, blankets, and tents. Bones and antlers became needles and knife handles and arrows.

But today, nobody needs a fur coat. There are fake furs that look and feel like the real thing. We can choose warm wool coats made without killing sheep or heavy leather coats that come from the hides of cows killed for steak and hamburger. We even have superwarm winter coats made with a filling that comes from recycled plastic soda bottles! So who wears fur? People who don't care very much about Earth!

Action #33. Be a Fur Foe

♦ Whenever you see someone in a fur coat, politely ask them if they know that animals died so they could be warm.

♦ Do stores in your local mall sell fur coats? Write a letter or draw a picture about selling animal fur and send it to the person who owns the store. Get your friends to do the same thing.

♦ Fur foes have a lot of protest marches in big cities. If you hear about one in a city near you, ask your parents if you can all go and march against fur, too.

Bird-o-Mat

Birds eat all day long. We hardly see them in the summer because there are plenty of their favorite foods around for them to eat: insects, grains, fruit, and worms. But in winter, deep snow and freezing temperatures make it hard for birds to find enough food to stay warm. That's where you come in.

Action #34. Start a Seed Squad

Turn your yard or window sill into a winter feeding station by making a birdfeeder out of fat, birdseed, and a mesh onion bag.

Step 1. Save an old mesh onion bag and buy some birdseed. Winter birds are wild about sunflower seeds, which have the most fats and oils in them. Get some suet (meat trimmings) from the butcher in your neighborhood. Trimmings usually end up in the garbage so you should be able to get them for free.

Step 2. Get a grown-up to help you melt the trimmings in a pan. When all the trimmings have become liquid fat, stir in the sunflower seeds.

Step 3. When the fat and seed mixture cools down, make a ball about the size of a grapefruit out of it. Your hands will get greasy, but the grease will wash off with soap and water.

Step 4. Place the ball into the onion bag. Use a piece of string to tie it tight.

Step 5. Tie the other end of the string to a tree branch or something tall that you can see from your window. Go back inside and wait. In a day—sometimes even less than a day—birds will find your seed station. Look for blue jays, chickadees, cardinals, and even woodpeckers. You'll have fun watching them, and you'll be helping them make it through the winter.

Starting Now

Kids who start taking care of animals today will grow up to be the first adults who really know what it means to be kind to all the animals!

Action #35. Become an Animal Activist

♦ Find out what animals are in trouble and what you can do to help. Every issue of *P3, The Earth-based Magazine for Kids* tells kids about one animal in trouble. P3 stands for Planet 3—that's Earth, the third planet from the sun. To get a sample copy of *P3*, send $2.00 to: *P3*, P.O. Box 52, Montgomery, VT 05470, or to: Trumpet Book Club, 666 Fifth Avenue, New York, NY 10103.

♦ Learn more about your favorite animals. Check out animal books at the library. The National Geographic Society has a whole library of videos about animals. Ask your video store owner if they are available. There's also a magazine that's all about nature—it's called *Ranger Rick*. Send $2.00 for a sample issue to: Ranger Rick, 8925 Leesburg Pike, Vienna, VA 22184.

♦ The next time you go to the zoo, talk to the zookeepers. They know a lot about the animals they take care of. They can tell you how the wild cousins of the animals you're looking at are doing. And most zoos have clubs that supply information on animals to their members. You can call your zoo to find out about joining. You'll find the phone number in the Yellow Pages under "ZOO."

Earth Actions

Know Your Planet!

There are two good reasons to get to know your planet.

1. It's an adventure.

2. It's a way to see for yourself that Earth is a planet worth saving.

There's a whole world on Earth that has nothing to do with shopping malls, report cards, and the latest hit video. It's a world of ocean tides, towering trees, and beautiful sunsets.

It's a world where anyone who's quiet and patient can watch a butterfly coming out of a cocoon, see a deer nibble at apples in a snow-covered yard, or hear an owl hoot on a starry summer night. It's a world that you belong to, too.

Action #36. Keep an Earth Journal

Start keeping track of nature in a notebook. Write down or draw everything you see around you that's not man-made. Making notes will really help sharpen your eyes so you can see nature all around you.

♦ Draw the trees and plants you see every day. Label the ones you know. Borrow a guide-book from the library to look up the rest.

♦ Note the animals, birds, and insects you see everyday. Do they play? Do they work all the time? Do they talk to each other? Jot your thoughts in your journal.

♦ Write down each day's weather. How do plants and animals react to changes in temperature and moisture? How does the natural world change along with the weather?

Hands On!

What do you like best that you can find only on Earth? Bright orange and red fall leaves? Seashells? Unusual rocks? Birdfeathers or birds' nests? Start an Earth collection of your favorite things. It's a way to get out into nature and show other people some of the things of beauty on our planet.

Action #37. Start a Collection

Step 1. Decide what your Earth collection will have in it. It's totally yours, so anything goes!

Step 2. Find a place in your house or room to store your collection. Use your Earth Journal (see Action #36) to keep track of what you find where.

Step 3. Show your collection to your friends. They'll see that you really like what you find here on Earth. They may want to start Earth collections of their own!

The Wild Report

A walk in the woods can be a lot more than good exercise. Animals leave lots of clues about where they've been and what they've done. But not many people can see them. That's because they don't know what to look for. See if you can train yourself to read the wilderness the way you would a book. Try it the next time you're in a forest or park.

Action #38. Take a Hike!

♦ When your family plans a vacation, see if you can spend a few hours walking in the woods in a national park or forest. Don't forget to take your Earth Journal!

♦ Stop at the ranger station and ask about the best places for a walk.

♦ When you're on the trail, look for grass and branches that have been nibbled on. Chances are a deer has made a meal there. If you see that bark has been scraped off a tree, a deer probably ate that, too.

♦ If a bird starts scolding you, look in nearby trees for its nest.

♦ Anything on the ground that looks like dirt pellets or marbles could be animal droppings. Poke them apart with a stick and you'll find signs of what the animal ate. If there are little bones or hairs, it could be owl pellets. Seeds or grain might mean deer. Fruit pits, bones, and seeds could be a raccoon.

♦ Check muddy spots for animal tracks. Draw them in your Earth journal and show the page to a ranger. Rangers can usually match tracks to animals.

♦ If you stop for a picnic, remember to take away any leftovers and garbage!

Natural Light

Light is made up of seven colors: red, orange, yellow, green, blue, indigo, and violet. We don't usually see all those colors separately because when they're blended together, we see them as sunlight. But when light passes through water, it breaks up into seven different color bands. The same thing happens with a prism—light rays are bent and separated.

Rainbows are nature's way of showing light's different colors. After a rainstorm, water droplets in the air catch and break the light into a huge arc of color. It's a light show you'll see only here on Earth, and you can make one yourself.

Action #39. Make Your Own Rainbow

♦ Take a garden hose and attach a nozzle that can spray a fine mist.

♦ Spray the water in front of you at an angle to the sun. You'll see a rainbow in the spray. That's because the water in the spray is bending the sunlight into its seven-color pattern.

Here's an added Earth Action: Spray the water in your garden. That way the plants get to drink in the water while you get to drink in the beauty!

Seed Scene, Part I

Every summer, plants and flowers send out seeds. That's how nature makes sure those types of plants will continue to grow on Earth. The wind is the main way seeds travel. Insects that brush against plants or eat their seeds also spread them. So do animals, and sometimes, so do you! You can see for yourself how many seeds there are all around.

Action #40. Plant Your Feet

Step 1. Take an aluminum pie tin and fill it almost to the top with dirt.

Step 2. Ask a grown-up to turn the oven on to 350 degrees. Place the tin of dirt in the oven for a half hour. This will kill any seeds already in the dirt.

Step 3. Put on some shoes or sneakers that have deep tracks on the bottom. Walk across some damp grass or a wettish field in early summer.

Step 4. When you get home, take your shoes off and scrape the dirt inside the tracks into your pie pan of dirt.

Step 5. Place it in the sun, water occasionally, and watch for something to grow!

Seed Scene, Part II

Growing seeds from packets is a fun way to see how easy it is to learn basic gardening skills.

Action #41. Plant Your Name—and Eat It!

Anyone can grow their name. All you need are two aluminum pie plates and a packet of cress seeds, which you can buy at any garden store.

Step 1. Wet a clean rag and place it in a pie plate. Then carefully pour cress seeds on the rag in the shape of the letters of your name.

Step 2. Cover the rag and seeds with the other pie plate.

Step 3. Every few days, take the top pie plate off and gently sprinkle the rag and seeds with water until the rag is wet. In a few days, you'll see your name start to sprout.

Step 4. Then take the top pie plate off for good and water the sprouts every three days.

Step 5. When the letters are big enough, add the sprouts to a peanut butter sandwich or a salad!

Plants Part I

Start your own garden. It's fun, easy, and a good way to see for yourself how things grow. You can do it indoors with houseplants and move outside in summer.

Action #42. Go Green!

♦ A great plant for beginners is a jade. It's beautiful to look at and easy to take care of. If you know anyone who has a jade plant, ask them for a clipping. That means snipping a small piece with some stem and leaves off the larger plant.

♦ Stick the stalk of jade in a pot of sandy soil. Place the pot in a place that's sunny sometimes but also gets some shade. Water until the dirt is damp, and let it grow. A jade doesn't need much water—once very two weeks is usually enough.

♦ As it grows, you can snip pieces off the plant and start some new ones by sticking the stems into the soil. They make great green gifts for other Earth fans.

Plants, Part II

Once you've mastered houseplants, it's time to move into the garden. This means taking what you've learned indoors outdoors.

Action #43. Try Tomatoes

Step 1. Start indoors around St. Patrick's Day. Take some of the compost you've been making (see Action #3), mix it with soil, and fill each egg slot in a cardboard egg carton.

Step 2. Use a pencil eraser to make a hole about ¼-inch deep in the dirt in each section. Drop one tomato seed into each hole. Cover the seeds with dirt and water them.

Step 3. Keep the egg carton on a sunny windowsill. Water the seeds enough to keep the surface moist. The seedlings will start to grow in about a week.

Step 4. When the second set of leaves appears, transplant the seedlings, dirt and all, into a larger pot. Keep watering them until mid-May.

Step 5. Prepare your garden. Choose a sunny spot where water doesn't puddle after a rainstorm. Chop up the dirt and toss any weeds onto your compost pile.

Step 6. Mix some rich compost in with the dirt. Plant your tomatoes about 1 foot apart. As they grow, you may want to tie the main stalk to a strong stick. This will help the plant stand up.

Use strips of rags instead of string for your ties—string will cut into the plant. Weed and water all summer, and you'll get 10 to 30 tomatoes from each plant!

Step 7. Make a spaghetti sauce with your tomatoes. Just put 12 to 15 clean tomatoes in a big pot with about a half inch of water on the bottom. Ask a grown-up to turn the stove on to a low heat. Add your favorite spices: salt, a little sugar, maybe some basil leaves. Simmer—that means cook slowly—for 4 hours. If you start at noon, you can have your own sauce for supper!

Bug Watch

There's no reason for gardeners to use toxic bug sprays. Why risk harming the groundwater and the people who'll eat the vegetables? Plenty of gardeners use natural ways to keep ahead of hungry insects. You can, too!

Action #44. Use Nature's Aid

♦ Hornworms and other bugs like to eat tomato leaves and flowers, but they can't stand marigolds. Marigolds are yellow and gold flowers that are natural tomato protectors. Plant a marigold next to every tomato plant to keep the munching bugs away.

♦ For double tomato protection, try planting dill along side the marigolds. Dill is a grassy plant that smells like dill pickles! After you harvest your tomatoes, harvest your dill, too. You can use it in dips, tomato sauce, and soups.

♦ Try this homemade spray to keep other insects away: You'll need 6 cloves of garlic, 1 onion, some red pepper, liquid soap (don't use dishwashing liquid), and a 1-gallon jar. Crush the garlic and chop the onion. Measure out a tablespoon of hot red pepper and 1 teaspoon of liquid soap. Mix the mash up with a gallon of hot water from the tap. Let it sit for a day. Then strain the chopped bits out.

Then find a plastic pump bottle—the kind that hand lotion or soft soap comes in. Wash it out well with warm water and soap. Then pour your homemade bug brew into it, and spray your plants to make bugs stay away.

"For Kids Only" Actions

Radical Reads

Here's a round-up of some great books and magazines about our home planet! Check them out of the library. . . and if you like them, tell your friends to read them, too!

Action #45. Check Them Out!

♦ *The Big Book for Growing Gardeners* by A. Vogel (Coppenrath Verlag, Münster, West Germany). This easy-to-read book is full of pictures and good advice for first-time gardeners. It even comes with packets of seeds in the back and a little spade to help dig up the soil! (Grade level: 2-3)

♦ *Where the Forest Meets the Sea* by Jeannie Baker (Greenwillow Books, NYC). The awesome art in this book shows a dad and his son spending the day on a beautiful beach near a tropical rainforest. (Grade level: 3-4)

♦ *The Usborne Book of Earth Facts* by Lynn Bresler (EDC Publishing, Tulsa, OK). Do you know what a *tsunami* is? What animal is the best mountain climber of all? These are just two tidbits you'll find in this fun and colorful book crammed with Earth information. (By the way, a *tsunami* is a huge wave made by an underwater volcano or an earthquake, and mountain goats are the best climbers of all!) (Grade level: 4-6)

♦ *The Nature Book* by Midas Dekkers (Macmillan, NYC). Any kid who spends the summer outdoors can have fun with this book. It shows how to weave baskets, make birdhouses, and a treehouse, and feed wild animals. (Grade level: 5-6)

♦ *P3, The Earth-based Magazine for Kids* is an eco-journal for kids. It's colorful, fun, and filled with action and addresses you can use to help save the planet. Send $2.00 for a sample issue to: P.O. Box 52, Montgomery, VT 05470. (See Action #52.)

♦ *Ranger Rick* magazine has stories, wonderful color photos, and fascinating facts about all kinds of animals. And there's a story every month about a raccoon named Ranger Rick! Send $2.00 for a sample issue to: Ranger Rick, 8925 Leesburg Pike, Vienna, VA 22184.

♦ *World* Magazine is filled with stories about people and animals that live all over the planet. The photographs are sensational! Send $2.00 for a sample issue to: *World* Magazine, National Geographic Society, Washington, D.C. 20036.

Radical Writes

Mail is one way to save the planet. Send letters to politicians, newspaper editors, company presidents, and anyone else you can think of. Tell whomever you write to what you're doing to save Earth. Ask them what *they're* doing.

You can never tell. Your letter might change someone's mind or make them see that it's up to *us* to save the planet.

Action #46. Start Writing Letters

Use these addresses to start with, and then find your own. And keep those cards and letters going!

♦ The President of the United States can lead the way to a cleaner, safer future for all of us. Tell the President what you think of Earth's problems. Send your letters to: President George Bush, The White House, 1600 Pennsylvania Avenue, Washington, D.C. 20501.

♦ Your Congressmen and women represent you in Washington. Let them know what you think needs to be done to save the planet. Send letters for your Representative to: United States House of Representatives, Washington, D.C. 20515. The Senate's address is: United States Senate, Washington, D.C. 20510.

♦ Letters to the editor are printed every day in almost every newspaper. The letters are a way for people in the community to express their opinions. Send your ideas about saving the planet to your local newspaper. You can find the address on the editorial page. You can usually find the page number of the editorial page in the table of contents.

Newspaper Headlines

Newspapers are full of stories about Earth, some good and some bad. Reading the headlines in the daily paper is the best way to find out who's helping and who's hurting Earth in your town. When you're finished with the daily newspaper, don't forget to recycle it.

Action #47. Clip and Send

Step 1. When your parents are finished with the newspaper, look on every page for headlines about Earth.

Step 2. Read the stories and cut them out.

Step 3. Tape each article about Earth to a piece of paper. Use that paper to write a letter to the person the story is about to let him or her know what you think! To find out where to mail it, call your newspaper. Ask for the reporter who wrote the story. The reporter can tell you where to send your letter.

Operation Earth Friend

Everybody counts when it comes to Earth Action. One of the best things you can do to help save the planet is to get a friend to help save the planet, too.

Action #48. Earth Wants You!

Choose a friend who's worried about pollution and animals in trouble. Let that person know that they can get in on the Earth Action today!

♦ Tell your friend what you're doing to help save the planet. Show your friend your letters to politicians. Tell him or her to write a letter, too!

♦ Show your pal your Daily Garbage Total (DGT). Explain how you're using it to break the throwaway habit. Maybe your friend will keep a DGT chart, too! (See Action #1.)

♦ Save the planet together! Choose any action from this book and do it with your friend. Talk about what else you can do for Earth as a team.

Talking Back

Many stores sell everything from soda pop to frozen yogurt in cups and dishes that can hurt the planet. It's almost impossible to eat out without ending up with plastic foam and plastic garbage. It's important to start speaking up in places that sell products that are bad for Earth.

Action #49. Speak Out for Earth!

♦ When you're in a fast-food restaurant, see if they'll bring your food in cardboard or paper containers instead of foam and plastic ones. Politely explain to the person taking your order that you want something that won't hurt the planet.

♦ Pack your own fork, knife, and spoon. Ask your mom for an old fork, knife, and spoon you can carry in your backpack. That way, you won't have to use plastic. Show them to the person serving you and politely tell him or her why you won't use plastic utensils anymore.

♦ Ask the server if the restaurant recycles any garbage or composts leftover salad-type food. If the answer is no, look for a suggestion box. Write your suggestions for ways the place can cut back its DGT and drop them in the suggestion box. If there is no suggestion box, ask for the manager's name and take down the restaurant's address. When you get home, write a letter to the manager.

Kids Count!

All over the U.S.A. kids are starting ecological clubs in school. They're getting together and acting as a team to make sure their school is doing its part to help save the planet. You can join them by starting a club in your school!

Action #50. Start an EcoKid Club

Step 1. Ask around and see how many kids in your class would join an Earth club. Have them ask their friends, too.

Step 2. When you know there are enough kids who want to help save the planet, choose a teacher everyone likes. Ask him or her to help you set up the club.

Step 3. Decide what day you'll meet. The teacher can usually get a classroom to use after school is over for the day.

Step 4. At the first meeting, decide what the school can do to help Earth. Choose three actions and talk about how to get started. Things schools can do include: using recycled paper, recycling all waste paper, starting a compost heap with cafeteria food, holding recycling drives, running a poster contest about ways to save the planet, raising money to adopt an acre of rainforest, hanging birdfeeders outside in winter.

Step 5. Give your club a cool name. Here are some suggestions: Eco Power, EKO (Earth Kids Organization), The Enviros. If you don't like these, think of your own.

Step 6. Publish a club newspaper and sell it in school. Tell other kids what they can do to help save Earth. Use the money you make to adopt an acre of rainforest or save a manatee or help the school buy recyclable trays for the cafeteria.

Step 7. Stick with it! Before the year is out, kid power will be making a difference!

Don't Live on Earth Without It!

Make an EcoCard that everyone in your family or Earth club carries. It's an exciting way to keep track of your Earth Actions—and it gets other people involved!

Action #51. Create Your Own EcoCard

Step 1. Decide on 10 Earth Actions everyone in the family, class, or Earth Action club should try to do in a month. An Earth Action could be "recycle 10 soda cans." Or "pick up 15 pieces of litter from the sidewalk." Or "plant a tree." Or "turn the water off while brushing your teeth."

Step 2. Decide on a reward for the person who does all 10 actions first. A packet of vegetable seeds is a great reward! So is a video rental of the winner's choice.

Step 3. Cut out pieces of cardboard in the shape of a credit card. Write EcoCard, or a name you like better, on the front. Draw a symbol for your card—a tree, a cow, anything you like—and color it in with crayon or colored pencil. (The ink in felt-tip markers is not that good for the environment.)

Step 4. Write the name of the cardholder on the front, too. Don't forget to leave a line for the cardholder's signature.

Step 5. List the 10 Earth Actions on the back. Put a check box next to each item on the list.

Step 6. Every time a member performs one of the Actions, he or she should check off that box.

Step 7. The first person to complete all 10 Earth Actions wins the prize.

Step 8. Issue new EcoCards every month. And don't forget to recycle your old ones!

Join the Third-Planet Team

There's a new magazine just for kids, and it's all about saving the planet. It's called *P3, The Earth-based Magazine for Kids*. Each issue of *P3* is filled with pictures, mazes, articles, and letters from kids around the United States that will help you understand what you can do month after month to help save the planet. (See Action #45.)

Action #52. Get Your Hands on *P3!*

A lot of school libraries already get *P3*. Look for it in your school. If you like it, ask your parents to order it for you.

P3 costs $14 for a year's subscription. To send for it, write to: *P3* Magazine, P.O. Box 52, Montgomery, VT 05470.